COLERAINE
and the
CAUSEWAY COAST
An Illustrated History and Companion

Paintings by
Gerald Maguire

Text by
Bob Curran B.A. Ph.D.

Cottage
Publications

First published by Cottage Publications,
Donaghadee N. Ireland 1995.
Copyrights Reserved
© Illustrations by Gerald Maguire 1995
© Text by Bob Curran 1995
All rights reserved.
Printed in Singapore

ISBN 0 9516402 8 3

List of Contents

The Artist

Born in Belfast in 1959, Gerald Maguire is a self taught artist who is equally comfortable working in oils or watercolours. Although he has painted scenes all over Ireland, he is most attracted to subjects along the Causeway Coast with a particular interest in buildings. Currently living in his native Belfast, his studio in Castlerock, which he opened for many years as a gallery during the summer months, is well known throughout the Coleraine and Causeway Coast area. Formerly employed as a draftsman with the Civil Service, the continually increasing demand for his work has recently permitted Gerald to become a full-time artist.

The Author

Born in the Mourne Mountains of County Down, Bob Curran has lived in the Coleraine area for over twenty years. A graduate of the University of Ulster at Coleraine, Bob was awarded a Ph.D. in Education in 1990. Married to a local girl, he has always taken a keen interest in the history and folklore of the region and has taught and written extensively on both topics. His voice is well known to radio listeners through his frequent presentation of items of local history and folklore and he also researched and scripted much of the background material for the Myths and Legends section of the Dunluce Centre in Portrush. Heavily involved in the development of Adult and Community Education, Bob has travelled widely and his services are always very much in demand, both as a lecturer on Irish History and folklore and as a storyteller.

Coleraine:–

"A Lady of Quality Amongst Towns"

Although no-one knows the exact meaning of the name Coleraine, it is generally accepted that it derives from the ancient Irish "Cuil Rathain" – the ferny corner. The Book of Armagh tells how a local Christianised chieftain offered Saint Patrick a site upon which to build a new church in 430 A.D. He pointed to a spot where some children were playing amongst a dense clump of ferns and the delighted saint used it as the location of his holy house. It was around this church that the original settlement of Cuil Rathain – probably no more than a few rude, thatched huts clustered in a river valley – grew.

The site of the settlement was very old even in those ancient times. Archaeologists have identified it as one of the oldest inhabited places in Ireland. At Mountsandal, on the southern outskirts of the town, traces of habitation have been uncovered, dating back to the Bronze Age and Neolithic and Mesolithic times.

The area all around was wild, boggy and heavily forested and was the domain of local "kings" who were little more than petty warlords and tribal chieftains. The northern coast was dotted with such small kingdoms – Dalriada Tuasceart (North Dalriada), Arachty O'Kahan (the country of the O'Cahans, west of the Bann) and Thua Inver (the territories around the mouth of the Bann – possibly around present-day Downhill) – each with its own ruler. The earliest of these kings that we know of was Niall of the Shining Deeds, ruler of Dalriada Tuasceart, who in 1 A.D. placed his sword into the hands of the Irish High King Connor MacNessa at Tara, as a token of his loyalty. Niall controlled the lands around Portrush and was only one of a number of kings in that area.

The original settlement of Coleraine was built close to the river crossing of Farsad Cambus, then the most northern ford on the Bann River. This is now known as Camus, about four miles south of the present town. Around 540 A.D. a monastery was founded there with Carbreus as its first bishop. This was replaced in 1244 by St. Mary's Friary, built a little further along the river. The new abbey was built in the protection of the Mountsandal fort, which gave it at least some protection from the conflicts which raged round about.

The important river-crossing and the monastery drew raiders of many descriptions who looted and pillaged the area. Most notable of these were the Vikings. In 932 A.D. both the Abbey and the settlement were completely burned to the ground and the Abbot Airmedach slain by the Danes of Lough Cuan (Strangford).

The most ferocious of all the Viking raiders, however, was Magnus Barefoot, King of Norway, whose warfleet dropped anchor off Portrush in September 1102. The northern coast had a reputation for fine cattle and Magnus demanded a tribute of 300 bullocks from the local inhabitants or else he would attack them. The local kings agreed but asked for three days grace to assemble the cattle. Magnus sailed up the Bann and attacked Coleraine and its Abbey, destroying the High Cross there and killing many of the monks. From the Abbey lands, he reputedly returned to Portrush to collect his cattle. The kings of the north coast, however, had no intention of giving him what he asked and had used the allotted time in assembling a war-band to attack him. As soon as the Vikings arrived, they were set upon and Magnus himself was killed at a place called the War Hollow (the site of the present golf-course). Completely routed, the raiders who were now commanded by Magnus's son, fled back to their ships. Before they left, they managed to hide the calf-skin of gold close to modern-day Portrush. If they intended to return and claim it, they never did and the fabulous treasure still lies there awaiting discovery.

In retaliation for the death of Magnus, his erstwhile ally Murkertah O'Brien, King of Munster – ravaged the entire coastline from Ballycastle to Downhill, slaughtering many of the inhabitants and killing several of the petty kings.

In 1315, following his defeat at Tannybrake near Ballymena, the Earl of Ulster took shelter in Coleraine from the pursuing Scots-Irish forces of Edward Bruce. Aided by certain Irish chieftains Bruce, the younger brother of the famous Robert, was trying to establish a Celtic kingdom in Ireland (with himself as ruler) but was meeting with fierce opposition from the Anglo-Normans already living there. Aided by Scottish pirates, he besieged Coleraine and many of the inhabitants were killed. Bruce went on to battles further south and was finally defeated and slain at Faughart, near Dundalk, by Sir John de Bermingham.

The history of Coleraine as a settled community really began in the mid 16th century. In 1534, Shane O'Boyle, the last prior of St. Mary's Abbey, surrendered the building and its lands to the commissioners of the English King, Henry VIII, and it was subsequently bought in 1604 by the English adventurer, Sir Thomas Phillips. It was Sir Thomas who built some 30 thatched cottages – homes for his workers – which were to form the embryo of Coleraine.

Encouraged by the Lord-Deputy, Sir Arthur Chichester who met with him in 1609, Phillips invited a number of London Companies to finance the building of a fortified Plantation town on the banks of the Bann. In 1610, a group consisting of a Governor, Deputy-Governor and 24 assistants (all from London companies) was formed to direct Plantation affairs and became known as "The Honourable the Irish Society".

Although Coleraine was growing, another town was rapidly becoming the administrative centre for a greater part of the area –

that was the town of Dunluce. Legend states that Dunluce Castle has stood on a headland looking towards Jura for almost one thousand years. Certainly, it was a Norman stronghold in the 13th century before falling under the control of the McQuillans who were said to have come to the area with William de Burgo, a Norman knight. The Castle and its lands were subsequently lost to the MacDonnells – a Scottish family following the Battle of Aura. A small town had grown up about the Castle walls and it was rapidly becoming a market centre for the locality. Indeed public executions were carried out there and the hill, just inland from the Castle itself where the road splits in two is known locally as Hangman's Hill and was the site of a local gallows. Tradition says that when the road itself was being built, the workmen were afraid to cut through the hill as it was 'a bad place' and so the division was brought about as a kind of compromise. Disease and the rapid development of Coleraine, may well have put paid to the expansion of Dunluce and it went into decline although some of the foundations of the old houses may still be seen.

In 1588, during an attempted invasion of England by Spain, a ship of the Spanish Armada – the galleas Girona, powered by both sail and oar – was wrecked off Dunluce Castle. The badly overladen vessel was carrying survivors from two other Spanish ships – the Ratara and the Santa Anna – who were trying to make the open sea beyond Dunluce headland and reach Scotland where they would receive a sympathetic welcome. Guided by pilots from North Donegal, the Girona limped past Dunluce late at night and in the teeth of a raging gale. Mistaking the lights of the Castle for those of another ship, the Spanish captain ordered his men to open fire. The MacDonnells of Dunluce returned fire, driving the galleas further out into the storm-tossed sea where she struck a reef at the mouth of the River Bush and sank almost immediately. Out of the crews of three ships, only five men survived and were received by Sorley Boy MacDonnell, then Lord of Dunluce and were subsequently allowed to proceed to Scotland. Bodies from the disaster were washed up along the coast for days after and many of them were buried in Dunluce churchyard. From the wreck Sorley Boy claimed items of gold, several casks of brandy and three Spanish cannons which were used in the defence of Dunluce for a number of years afterwards.

In 1611, the first dwellings of the new town of Coleraine, surrounded by high earthen ramparts, began to rise on the Bann. These stout timber-frame houses, featuring brick chimneys, were made from wood hewn in the forest south of the Sperrin Mountains, filled with wooden cross-pieces and then plastered. These first houses were referred to as "The New Row", a name which survives to this day. The town was surrounded on all sides by an earth wall with two gates – the King's Gate at one side and the Blind Gate at the other. The ramparts ran from the shores of the Bann, around St. Patrick's Church, returning to the river through what is now Society Street (part of this street was still referred to as "the oul' rampart" by elderly people as late as this present century). Within the safety of these walls, the townspeople could graze their animals on "the long acre" (a stretch of common ground in the south-east of the town). This is still called "Long Commons".

The Bann served as a centre for industry in the emerging town. Along its banks were to be found a malting-house, a brew-house, a large work-yard and a brick and tile house. The Mill, after which Mill Street is named, was old even in the 17th century, when it milled wheat and made malt. The brook which supplied the mill-dam gave its name to Brook Street close by.

It was whiskey which was the main export of the town. In 1608, King James I granted a patent for distilling spirit in the Coleraine area but it was known that "acqua vitae" (whiskey) had been illegally made in the locality for generations before. It was distilled as far away as Port Cammon (Bushmills) where "the sweet waters from

Knocklayd give it a very pleasant and commendable taste". Coleraine whiskey was widely savoured amongst the gentry of the day and continued to be so right across the centuries. An old song from around the mid 19th century says:

"The Spaniard may boast of his sherry,
The Frenchman, his sparkling champagne,
But if a man wants to be merry,
I'd advise him to try 'Old Coleraine'"

Another important industry around the developing town of Coleraine was tanning. One of the foremost tanneries in the area flourished near the town between the years 1612-1618. It was owned by Richard Fitzsimons, a Drogheda merchant, who had set up a tannery on the outskirts of the town. Fitzsimons seems to have been an important man in the early days of Coleraine because, together with Oliver Nugent of Ballyness, he controlled the salmon fisheries on the Bann. Records for June 1615 show that he exported tanned hides to Spain and by the following August sales were £657 in one month alone – a considerable sum for those days. In 1618, he obtained a licence to build a bigger tanhouse at the Dogleap, near the developing settlement of Newtownlimavady (Limavady) and he moved his premises there. He was not, however, the only tanner in the area. John Rowley of Coleraine also exported tanned hides to London. Rowley was the Irish Agent for the London Companies and owned a brew-house and tannery in the village of Castleroe, south of the town. For a while there was a good market for Coleraine hides but, with the improvement of relations between Spain and England and a demand for Spanish leather, local trade began to fall away.

Coleraine was also a market town – its market being held on the site of the current Diamond. Country people would sometimes travel to the town across the Bann, often approaching by means of a ferry – giving rise to the now vanished right of way known as Ferryquay

Street. As the market grew and expanded, a new location had to be found for it. A site near the Blind Gate was chosen – what was to become the Market Yard – and Dirty Lane which connected this market to the centre of the town became known as Newmarket Street.

In the early 18th century, two towns existed – one within the earthen walls and another on the far shore of the Bann. The houses which had grown up on the western shore, outside the town ramparts, took their name from an old church. In the 12th century, a castle had been built beside the river and was given the name Drumtarsy Castle. A church – St. Eugene's – was built in 1288 to serve it and gave its name to the surrounding parish. In old Irish, this was known as Cill Eogain (the Church of Eugene) which was gradually anglicised into its present name of Killowen. The area was generally referred to as "the Castle-side of the river" but as the castle itself decayed and eventually had to be pulled down, the description held less meaning and the name was changed to the Waterside. Gradually, streets began to appear as this town grew – Captain Street and Killowen Street being the principal ones. As Coleraine expanded, Killowen was incorporated into the town, although many in the Waterside district still consider themselves to be distinctive from those living on the other side of the river.

Having received its Charter of Incorporation in 1613, Coleraine also became a garrison town. Soldiers were quartered in Barrack Street (now Bridge Street) and were used for the defence of the northern coastline against foreign invasion and local insurrection.

The borough was not always the well-paved and tidy place that it is today. Early reports of the London Commissioners declare that the "streets are in a filthy state, uneven and barely passable". Nevertheless, the money of the London Companies soon rectified the situation and later descriptions of the town describe it as "a trim borough – a lady of quality amongst towns".

The upheavals of the Irish Rebellion of 1641 did not leave the area unscathed. In 1642 Coleraine was once again attacked by Catholic militia under the command of James MacColl MacDonnel ("James of the Glens") and James Oge McHenry O'Cahan. They were aided by Manus Roe O'Cahan of Castleroe.

On Friday, 11th February 1642, six hundred Protestants and three hundred English soldiers marched from the town to engage with a Catholic army under Alister MacDonnel, marching north from Ballymoney. These forces met at a place called the Laney and the Catholics were victorious, giving no quarter and slaughtering most of the Protestant forces. Protestants from the surrounding locality fell back to Coleraine which was then besieged. James MacDonnel established a base at Cloughfin (now Cloyfin) and called on the town to surrender. Under the leadership of Archibald Stewart and Edward Rowley, the town held out, although in the grip of starvation and disease, awaiting the arrival of General Munroe and the Covenanting Army of Scotland who were marching from Carrickfergus. When Munroe arrived, he relieved the town and exacted a terrible revenge by decimating the surrounding Catholic lands and by burning the castle of Manus Roe O'Cahan. In May 1642, he defeated and massacred a Catholic army at Magilligan returning to Coleraine in order to appoint his son, Colonel George Munroe as garrison commander to ensure no further risings in the immediate area. The events of February 1642, however, were not forgotten and the date was long referred to locally as "Black Friday". In March 1689, Coleraine was once again threatened by a Catholic army, this time commanded by James II of England on its way to the siege at Derry. One of the commanders, Sir Arthur Rowdon, described the attack:

> "(They) appeared before our ramparts and advanced to within
> 50 yards of them under the shelter and covert of hedges and
> ditches which particular interest had hindered us from throw-

ing down. It was on the Blind Gate side and near the church, the mill sheltered them within 50 yards of the bastion".

The attack was unsuccessful and a month later, Sir Tristram Beresford raised a regiment of volunteers from the town to help the beleaguered defenders of Derry against the Catholic forces besieging the city. After the Williamite Wars, Coleraine became an important military post in the north, its commanders charged with ensuring that stability remained in the coastal countryside.

During the late 18th and early 19th century, the main prosperity of the area lay in linen. Brown linen products from Coleraine and Ballymoney were adjudged to be the finest in all Ireland. In 1752, the manufacture of linen prevailed mainly in the townlands of Ballyrashane and Ballywillan providing much employment for local people – a census poll for the Parish of Ballyrashane in 1764 records 213 weavers and 766 spinners living in the area. By 1854, the great bleachworks at Mullaghmore, Aghadowey, was one of the six largest of such concerns within the United Kingdom. In 1870, however, local trade was experiencing a slump and the Aghadowey works had gone into liquidation.

Starvation, fever and dysentery swept the local area as the linen trade fell away. Although the area had been spared the worst of the Irish Potato Famine in 1845-50, poverty was equally devastating on the community. A record of the bequests of the Aghadowey and Agivey Poor Relief Fund, which had been set up to counteract the worst of the linen slump, tell a pitiful tale:

> "James Shirla (Culcrow): a good weaver and an old man who is unwell, will not ask for more if possible.
>
> Benjamin Mitchell (Knockaduff): weakly and unable to work – a weaver.

William Martin (Cullycapple): now very ill – asks for money to get rations for four persons.

Betty Collins (Knockaduff): a spinner – attending her sister's children who are all ill with fever".

The Coleraine Workhouse was built in 1841 and was opened to inmates in April 1842. It was not left untouched by the diseases which were sweeping through the area and by April 1847, smallpox, dysentery, measles and fever were widespread there. The neighbouring area surrounding the town of Garvagh was also heavily infected and in 1855 a plague of cholera swept through the Waterside, perhaps brought in by the boats which traded along the Bann. The effects of this were devastating upon the community with over 80 persons dying and hundreds more suffering the effects of disease. Despite sickness and poverty, Coleraine itself and the surrounding districts continued to grow and expand. In July 1863, the town entered "The Age of Steam" as the the first railway link was established with Derry. Two years later, came the line from Belfast. Prior to this, all transport to and from the town had been by stagecoach. Coaches from Derry, Belfast and Dublin arrived daily, drawing up at inns such as "The Swan", the "Queen's Arms" or at "Nancy Price's" in Portrush. In 1834, a new coastal road had been built between Portrush and Portstewart to allow travellers to experience the breathtaking coastal scenery which accompanied their journey. The new railway brought travellers and tourists to the northern coast, mainly for holidays and to view natural wonders such as the Giant's Causeway.

The local people were not slow to exploit the local scenery and the railway line was quickly extended to Portrush. Portstewart, however remained slightly aloof from the commercial era and local landowners insisted that its railway station be built a little way outside the town, to discourage the working-class day-trippers from Belfast and to draw only people of 'quality'. Portrush, however, continued to bustle with tourists, becoming "the Blackpool of the North Antrim coast", a reputation which it continued to enjoy right up until the 1960's. The town had two large hotels, most prominently the Antrim Arms which was adjudged to be one of the most prestigious in all the North of Ireland and was widely used by judges, nobility and "persons of quality". This subsequently became the Northern Counties Hotel which was destroyed by fire in 1989.

The development of Coleraine continued apace. Spared the emigration which characterised many other Irish towns, by 1891 the population of the town was 6 854 and was still rising. New buildings were appearing, reflecting some of the best architecture of the day. In 1860, Coleraine Academical Institution was opened, taking its place with some of the finest educational establishments in Ireland; in 1852, the Courthouse was built and continued in service until a number of years ago.

Coleraine has always been a town loyal to Sovereign and country. On 21st September 1912, Sir Edward Carson addressed a crowd of 5 000 in the grounds of the Manor House of Coleraine and warned that a Civil War would sweep through Ulster. His speech inspired the development of a fully-trained Volunteer Force in the town – many of whom would fight in the Great War of 1914-18 in the Ulster Division. Many of them laid down their lives at the Battle of the Somme. After 1916, as unrest swept through Ireland, Coleraine was spared both disturbance and outrage – perhaps as a recompense for her earlier, more turbulent past.

In the relative calm of the town, people could enjoy themselves. Coleraine hosted the annual Bann Regatta which incorporated the Irish Amateur Rowing Cup – the Blue Riband of Irish rowing. Teams came from Limerick, Dublin, Drogheda, Portadown, Belfast and Derry to compete for this prestigious accolade. When the competition was over, there was dancing by gaslight in the Boat Club down by the river and whilst cannons roared in France, strollers along the Waterside could hear the sounds of a band playing 'Roses of Picardy' and 'If You Were the Only Girl' wafting across the river on a summer's night.

During the 1920s the affairs of the town were in the hands of the Urban Council which had replaced the old Town Commissioners, but in 1929 Coleraine was granted a new Charter and became a Borough.

Throughout the Depression which characterised the 1930s, she continued to grow. In 1937, the population was 9180 and out of 2118 houses in the town, only 56 were uninhabited.

During the Second World War, the settled status of Coleraine drew both soldiers and refugees. American soldiers were billeted in Coleraine and it became a great pastime for the children of the town to dive into the 'swimming lake' (now part of Railway Road) for money tossed in by the G.I.s. The Lombard Cafe in Queen Street became their store and it was said that there were many romances between local girls and visiting American troops.

With the War over, the town began to expand at an alarming rate. By the 1950s, the population has swollen to over 10000 and there was a housing shortage. The neighbouring towns of Portrush and Portstewart began to develop to take the overspill. The population of the three towns grew even more when, in 1968, Coleraine became a university town with the construction of the New University of Ulster overlooking the Bann on the Cove Hill at Ballysally. In 1984, the New University merged with the Ulster Polytechnic to form the University of Ulster, one of the largest and fastest growing educational institutions in the United Kingdom.

Despite this expansion, the town's troubles were still not over. In November 1992, a terrorist bomb destroyed the entire centre of the town, demolishing several shops and damaging the Town Hall. Since then, rebuilding work has been going on and it is a tribute to the industry and courage of the Coleraine people that a new and attractive town centre is now starting to emerge. It is due to the indomitable spirit of its people that Coleraine will once more become "a lady of quality amongst towns".

Main Events in the History of Coleraine

7000 B.C. Earliest known settlement in the area at Mountsandal.

1 A.D.   Niall of the Shining Deeds, King of Dalriada Tuasceart, swears allegiance to Connor McNessa at Tara.

430   St. Patrick offered land to build a church (the ferny corner).

504   Foundation of a Christian abbey at Farsad Cambus.

904   Bec Leathlobher, renowned Chief of Thua Inver (the territories around Downhill) dies.

930   Cuil Rathain burned by Danes of Strangford Lough.

1005   Brine, Son of Kennedy, invades Dalriada Tuasceart.

1015   Battle of Farsad Cambus between Dalriadans and Ulidians from County Down and occupation of area by the latter.

1102   Death of Magnus Barefoot, King of Norway, at Portrush.

1198   English settlers at Coleraine muster 300 men and march against the Irish king Aodh O'Neill at Larne.

1221   Coleraine destroyed by Manus MacDunlevy of Down.

1244   St. Mary's Dominican Abbey established at Coleraine.

1262   Peter O'Hetheren gives his name to the Parish of Agherton.

1315   The Earl of Ulster besieged at Coleraine by the forces of Edward Bruce of Scotland.

1534   Shane O'Boyle surrenders the Abbey building and lands during the Dissolution of Monasteries.

1584   Lord Deputy of Ireland, Sir John Perrot, proposes the building of a fortified town on the River Bann.

1588   Spanish galleas "Girona" wrecked off Dunluce Castle.

1604   Coleraine Abbey and lands bought by Sir Thomas Phillips.

1610	London Companies 'The Honourable The Irish Society' agree to finance the building of a town on the Bann.
1611	First houses built in Coleraine at New Row.
1639	Part of Dunluce Castle falls into the sea.
1641	General Munroe destroys castles all along the north coast.
1689	Coleraine threatened by a Jacobite army under King James.
1696	Mary Murphy – the famous Portrush giantess – appears before William III and Mary II in England.
1790	Lieutenant Stewart from Donegal founds Portstewart.
1810	The popular song "Kitty of Coleraine" written.
1832	Cholera epidemic sweeps Coleraine.
1834	The O'Hara family build a "castle" at Portstewart and a coastal road is built between Portrush and Portstewart.
1860	Coleraine Academical Institution opens.
1863	Railway line to Derry opens.
1912	Sir Edward Carson addresses the people of Coleraine.
1914	Volunteers from Coleraine join the Ulster Division of the British Army.
1929	Coleraine receives a new Charter and is a Borough.
1937	Population of the town almost 10000.
1950	Expansion of Portrush and Portstewart
1968	Coleraine becomes a university town.
1984	New University merges with Ulster Polytechnic.
1992	Terrorist bomb devastates centre of the town.
1995	Town centre rebuilt.

Gerald Maguire

Name and Address	Telephone

COLERAINE TOWN HALL

The Town Hall in the Diamond is certainly one of Coleraine's most imposing features. In the 17th and early 18th centuries, the Diamond was the main market place of Coleraine and a market-house, designed by an architect named Dance, was built on the site to oversee the commerce of the town. This also served as a communal meeting house and a town hall. The present Town Hall was built in 1859 on the site of that market-house at a cost of £4146, a not inconsiderable sum in those days. It was designed by Thomas Turner and contains many typical Turner features – horizontal rustication on the ground floor and baroque features in the surrounds to the windows.

With thanks to Todd Gallery

Gerald Maguire

B

ST. PATRICK'S WELL AND PORTSTEWART STRAND

Tradition has it that when St. Patrick built a church at Portstewart, he also blessed a local well which acquired healing properties and became a place of pilgrimage, raising revenue for the attendant church. The first note of this church and well appears in the tithe rolls of 1262 as "the church and well of O'Heatheran". From around 1790 a fair was held on Portstewart's beautiful strand on the first Monday in August. Known as 'Lammas Monday', old religious strictures forbade sheep, horses or cattle to be sold at it but it served as a holiday for the youths of the district. A notable feature of the fair (which continued until the late 1800's) was a horse-race along the magnificent strand.

With thanks to McIntyre's

Gerald Maguire

Name and Address	Telephone

ARCADIA BALLROOM, PORTRUSH

Nowhere in North Antrim more deserved the title "Ballroom of Romance" than the Arcadia on the East Strand, where many a holiday romance began to the music of the popular dance bands of the day. In 1900 this area was the Ladies Bathing Pool (from which men were excluded) but the bathing soon became mixed and R. A. Chalmers opened the Arcadia Tearooms to provide refreshments to bathers. A dance floor was soon added and the Arcadia grew in reputation reaching its heyday during the show-band era in the 50's, 60's and early 70's. However by the 1980's dance halls all over the country were in decline and by the end of the decade the Arcadia too had closed its doors.

With thanks to Grahams Gift Shop, Portrush

Gerald Maguire

Name and Address	Telephone

MAGHERABUOY HOUSE

Now a superbly appointed international hotel overlooking the splendours of the Causeway Coast, Magherabuoy was originally designed in 1860 by Charles Lanyon (who also designed Queens University) for Robert Hamilton M.D. of Liverpool who selected this magnificent site for his retirement home. The new mansion replaced a earlier house which had been on the site since the 17th century. Legend has it that a cobbler named McManus was given the surrounding land (known as Glenmanus) in return for shoeing General Munroe's army with a cart load of boots in 1642 when it was on its way to attack Portrush. He built the original house on this site with the rents he received for these lands.

With thanks to the Magherabuoy House Hotel

Gerald Maguire

Name and Address	Telephone

BUSHMILLS CLOCK TOWER

The ancient name for the settlement of Bushmills was Portcammon ('the herring port') as it was near there that the Anglo-Irish fishing boats unloaded their catches. The site of the town, however, was also historically significant since it was the crossing on the River Bush of the old chariot-road between the ancient Irish capital of Tara and the pre-Christian fortress at Dunseverick. One of the most striking features of the town's Market Square is the clock-tower. This was erected in 1874 by the local landowners – the McNaghten family – as part of an ornamental surround to the (then enclosed) Bushmills market. It is the only piece of the original ornamentation which survives to this day.

With thanks to Lindsay Shanks

Gerald Maguire

F

Name and Address	Telephone

ANDERSON PARK AND FOUNTAIN

This attractive open area lies close to the very centre of Coleraine and is named after its donor – Hugh Anderson J.P. The fountain (now sadly gone) was constructed by Walter McFarlane and Co. of Glasgow and erected in 1911. It was covered by a pretty cast iron dome (still standing) set on eight columns. An elegant ornamental heron (now also gone) sat on top of the fountain. The road intersecting the park originally swept in a curve from the harbour, along the edge of the town ramparts and back to the harbour again. It was used by merchants taking produce to and from boats and is still known as Circular Road, although it was also popularly known as the Horse Road.

With thanks to Coleraine Garden Centre

Gerald Maguire

Name and Address	Telephone

CASTLEROCK PRESBYTERIAN CHURCH

The earliest houses in the picturesque village of Castlerock probably date from around 1840, some 30 years before the Presbyterian Church was erected in 1870. The memorial tower was added in 1885 in memory of Samuel McCurdy Greer, the first Liberal M.P. for the county of Londonderry and a founder elder of the congregation there. The Manse, situated just opposite the church, was erected for the first minister – the Reverend Doctor William Irwin. The Reverend Irwin had a large family, even by the standards of the time – 10 children in all – and so 10 bedrooms were provided at the Manse.

THE IRISH SOCIETY SCHOOL

In 1705, the Coleraine Corporation wrote to The Honourable The Irish Society asking for help to establish a school. In response to this request the Society approved a scheme for a free school and a schoolhouse was established in 1707 near the centre of the town. In 1821 demand for schooling was so great that, financed partly by private subscription and partly by the Society, a larger school was built on the present site. Demand for places was so great that 400 children had to be refused admission. This original school was replaced by the present building which opened in 1869, continuing the reputation of academic excellence carried on by the schools and university in the town today.

With thanks to The Honourable The Irish Society

Gerald Maguire

I

Name and Address   Telephone

The Cutts and Mountsandal

The Gazetteer of Ireland (1844) described Mountsandal as 'a fine earthen work or Danish mound, one of the largest in the kingdom'. However it is certainly much older than the Danes who raided along the Bann – in fact archaeolgists have discovered traces of habitation there dating back to around 7–8000 B.C. making it one of the oldest known inhabited places in Ireland. The Cutts below takes its name from cuts made in the rock by John Rowley of Castleroe to allow the transportation of timber over the weir at Ballyness. The timber was used in the construction of Coleraine and the stone taken from the Cutts was used in the construction of Stone Row in the town.

With thanks to Tweedy Acheson

Gerald Maguire

Name and Address   Telephone

PORTRUSH PROMENADE AND HARBOUR

The original name for Portrush was 'Bo Rhinn' (the cow's point) and it was said to be the best area for rearing cattle in the whole of North Antrim. The waters between the Skerry Islands and the mainland were used by shipping as a calm and safe anchorage and gradually a town grew up along the shore taking the name 'Portrush' and becoming known as "the sheltered port". Portrush was the home of the most famous of all Irish giantesses Mary Murphy. Born in the town around 1670, Mary was reported to be both very tall (seven foot, two inches without shoes or headgear) and also very good-looking. She was presented at the court of King William III and Mary II in 1696.

With thanks to Morelli Cappuccino's (Portrush)

Gerald Maguire

Name and Address	Telephone

ST. JOHN'S ROMAN CATHOLIC CHURCH

During the Penal Times in Ireland, the laws forbidding Catholics to practice their religion were rigorously enforced in the area of Coleraine. Nevertheless, Catholics continued to meet and worship in secret and there is evidence from the time of services conducted at a Mass Rock and also of a Mass Walk in the Somerset Forest, south of the town. In 1760, during times of greater toleration, a Roman Catholic Church was built at the Burnside, near Chapelfield House. This was replaced in 1806 with a church at Kyle's Brae, although this had to be taken down because land slippage had made it dangerous. The present gothic style church was built close to the same site in 1834.

Gerald Maguire

Name and Address	Telephone

PORTBALLINTRAE STRAND

The small seaside village of Portballintrae has long been a favourite destination for summer visitors. The surrounding cliffs have a number of picturesque caves, some of which can only be approached from the sea. In times past these caves were used as storage for contraband (such as poteen and tobacco) which was landed along this coast by smugglers from Scotland and later sold in the markets of Ballymoney and Coleraine. Legend states that Runkerry Cave near Portballintrae was the final resting place of Finn McCool, builder of the Giants Causeway. The sound of the sea in these caves is supposed to reflect the sighs of the giant, weeping for the sins of the world.

With thanks to the Beach House Hotel

Gerald Maguire

Name and Address   *Telephone*

OLD BUSHMILLS DISTILLERY

In 1608, during the reign of King James I, the Distillery at Bushmills became the first in the world to be granted a licence to distil whiskey. Although today's technology permits greater control, the whiskey making process at Bushmills has remained unchanged since distilling was first practiced. The fame of 'Old Bushmills' whiskeys continues to spread throughout the world and the various brands produced by the Distillery can be found throughout all five continents. Many visitors enjoy their first taste of Bushmills whiskey after a tour of the Distillery which has become one of Northern Ireland's leading tourist attractions.

With thanks to Old Bushmills Distillery

Gerald Maguire

Name and Address	Telephone

BANN BRIDGE

From earliest times, Coleraine was the most important northerly crossing on the Bann. The original crossing may well have been by boat or ferry but, at some stage, a permanent bridge was established. There is some dispute about when the first bridge was erected. Some historians claim evidence of a stone bridge built in 1248 by Edmund Butler and there are references to a wooden bridge, built in the early 17th century, which could be partially raised, like a drawbridge. Certainly a wooden bridge existed around 1625 to connect Coleraine with a market which took place in Killowen each Saturday and a stone bridge (preceeding the present one) was in operation by 1673.

With thanks to H. Wilson Gordon & Co.

Gerald Maguire

Name and Address	Telephone

GIANT'S CAUSEWAY

Perhaps the best known Northern Irish landmark throughout the world, according to legend it was constructed by the Irish giant Finn McCool in an attempt to reach another mighty giant in Scotland, who likewise began to build a similar causeway in order to reach Ireland. The two met in the middle and their battle destroyed much of the now-completed crossing. Its true origins, however, have nothing to do with giants but with volcanic activity. Lava flowing from vents in the ground cooled in contact with the atmosphere, contracting and cracking to form the famous stone columns which have long been a source of wonder for visitors and tourists from all over the world.

With thanks to O. B. Video Productions

Gerald Maguire

Name and Address
Telephone

COLERAINE ACADEMICAL INSTITUTION

Today Coleraine Inst. is one of the most prestigious educational establishments in the Province, a reputation built up over a period of almost 150 years. The first proposals for an academical institution in the town were made in 1846 but, due to the Irish Famine, were laid aside until 1853 when a site was donated for the building by the Clothworkers Company. A prize of £20 was offered for the best design to include 'Dining and Common Halls, 2 schoolrooms, a museum, a laboratory and a schoolmaster's house'. The competition was won by Isaac Farrell and the school was completed in April 1860, although at £4000 the building cost twice as much as the original estimate allowed.

With thanks to Bookends

Gerald Maguire

Name and Address	Telephone

SCONCE AND MURDER HOLE ROAD

The Sconce is one of the most easterly eminences in a group of mountains separating north-east and north-west Ulster. Legend states that it was once a fortress belonging to Cetheren, a grandson of Niall of the Nine Hostages and that two kings were burnt there around 600 A.D. The area was well known as the main coaching-road between Coleraine and Limavady and, in the late 1700's, as the haunt of the notorious highwayman and murderer, Cushy Glen. He was shot on this road in 1804 and his body was taken to Limavady for public display. There is no real Murder Hole in this area and the name itself may have been taken from a famous murder site near Merrick in Galloway.

With thanks to Old Ballyness Cottages, Bushmills

Gerald Maguire

Name and Address

Telephone

Name and Address	Telephone

MUSSENDEN TEMPLE

Standing at the cliff edge at Downhill, Mussenden Temple was built by the Earl Bishop who resided at Downhill Castle. Although not married, the Bishop was very fond of the children within his family. He had a full cousin named Henrietta who had married James Bruce and the Bishop was very much attached to her children (her son, Harry Bruce, inherited the Bishop's Irish estates). Her daughter, Frideswide Bruce, was a particular favourite of the Bishop and shortly after she married Daniel Mussenden in 1781 the Bishop ordered the construction of the Temple in her honour. However she did not enjoy it long as she died in 1785, two years after the Temple was completed.

With thanks to Coleraine Books and News

Gerald Maguire

Name and Address	Telephone

ST. PATRICK'S CHURCH OF IRELAND

The original church was erected as a place of worship by the Irish Society in 1614, allegedly on the site where St. Patrick founded his monastery. This claim is hotly disputed by some who argue that the monastery lay in Killowen. An aisle was added to the building in 1684 as well as a wooden spire which was destroyed by lightning during a storm in 1719. In 1884, under an enthusiastic rector named Henry O'Hara, the church was almost entirely rebuilt by Thomas Drew R.H.A. who replaced the old tower with the current spire which soars above the church. At the same time, he raised the nave and added a clerestory and a north aisle.

Gerald Maguire

Name and Address	Telephone

CARRICK-A-REDE ROPE BRIDGE

This spectacular rope bridge connects a small off-shore island to the main-land and can only be safely crossed during the summer months. Legend states that at one time female hostages were left on the the island for the Vikings, who plundered this coast during the 9th-12th centuries, in the hope that the settlements along the coast would be spared. The unfortunate victim would be deposited on the island, a bridge would be drawn back and she would be left to the mercy of the raiders who approached from the sea. The last such tribute left is said to have been the King of Rathlin's daughter, freed by Cuchullain, who slaughtered the Viking pirates.

With thanks to Insurance and Travel

Gerald Maguire

Name and Address	*Telephone*

PORTRUSH STATION

The extension of the railway line from Coleraine in 1865 heralded a whole new era for Portrush. The new link to Belfast allowed tourists to flood into the town in great numbers and local people were not slow to take advantage with hotels and boarding houses quickly springing up to establish the town as a much sought-after holiday destination. In the early part of this century private carriages belonging to the hotels of the area would meet the trains to whisk the arrivals away to their lodgings for the holiday of a lifetime. Today's transport is more likely to be by car than by train but each year thousands of holiday makers still come "up to the Port" for their eagerly anticipated summer break.

With thanks to Fantasy Island

Gerald Maguire

Name and Address	Telephone

LIONS GATE

This is the main entrance to Downhill Castle which was destroyed by fire in 1851. The Castle was built in 1779 by Frederick Hervey, Bishop of Derry and third son of the First Earl of Bristol who seems to have been a colourful character with an eye for the ladies. It is rumoured that he courted every great beauty of the day including Madam Ritz, mistress of the King of Prussia and Lady Hamilton, who is famous for her association with Lord Nelson. He died on a journey from Albano to Rome on July 8th, 1803 and his body was packed and shipped back to England as an antique statue – a device of which the Earl Bishop, as he was known, would no doubt have approved.

With thanks to Gilpin Farm Machinery

Gerald Maguire

Name and Address   *Telephone*

COLERAINE METHODIST CHURCH

In 1772, the first Methodist preacher visited Coleraine and in 1778, Alexander Boyle rented a wing of the old army barracks which was converted into a small hall. This played host to a great Methodist expansion in the town spurred on by numerous visitations by John Wesley who visited Coleraine in 1778, 1785, 1787 and 1789. A new site for the meetings was obtained in 1799 and a new Church and a Manse were built in 1801/2. The church was constructed on the town rampart and cost £500. In time this church proved too small for the expanding congregation and the present church, designed in the classic corinthian temple style by Isaac Farrell, was opened in 1853.

Gerald Maguire

Name and Address	Telephone

PORTSTEWART CONVENT, DOMINICAN COLLEGE

Portstewart grew out of a grant of land given to one Peter O'Hetheran in 1259 and for a long time was known as "Bally O'Hetheran" (O'Hetheran's town). The town-site may well have been around what is now the Flowerfield area and it is possible that gentlemen of the district had their houses there. The village of Portstewart did not exist until 1790 and takes its name from a Colonel Stewart who came from Donegal. In 1834, a local landowner, Henry O'Hara, built a grand house on Portstewart headland locally nicknamed "The Castle". In 1917 the building was acquired by the Dominican Sisters who turned it into a convent and more latterly, a grammar school.

With thanks to Morelli's of Portstewart

Gerald Maguire.

Name and Address	Telephone

FLOWERFIELD HOUSE

The present house was built around 1830 by Samuel Orr, on the site of a ruined 17th century grange farm, the stables of which are still standing. It was owned for a time by Colonel Monroe, former Governor of Mountjoy Prison and brother of the famous writer H.H. Monroe ('Saki'). Legend has it that, in 1761, it served as a hiding place for the notorious highwayman and murderer, John MacNaghten ('Half-Hanged MacNaghten'). Tradition says that whilst soldiers were searching the house, MacNaghten (who was a handsome rogue) hid under the skirts of some ladies who were seated for afternoon tea and so avoided capture. His ghost is still said to haunt the stables and outhouses.

With thanks to McAfee Properties

Gerald Maguire

Name and Address	Telephone

DUNLUCE CASTLE

The name Dunluce is probably derived from the ancient Irish 'Dun Laois' (the strong fort). Tradition says that it was built by a chieftain named McKeown in order to 'awe his neighbours and terrorise the Caledonians across the water'. It was more properly originally built by the Normans who came to the area around the 12th century. Situated on an imposing headland, the castle is not the impregnable fortification which it might at first seem. Although well defended from the sea it was vulnerable to attack from the land behind. This was exploited in 1565 when Shane O'Neill's forces successfully besieged the castle. In 1639, part of the vast kitchens fell into the sea, killing 19 servants.

With thanks to Bishops Footwear Ltd.

Gerald Maguire

Name and Address	Telephone

OLD COURTHOUSE

From the late 17th century onwards, Coleraine became the main centre for administrative justice for the area. During the late 18th century, highway robbery and burglary became a problem in the area between Limavady and Coleraine and many of those involved were brought for trial in Coleraine. Famous among these were two members of the Joseph Scott gang who had been captured near Dungiven. Their public hanging was marked by the tolling of the town bell in Bellhouse Lane. Over the years there have been several courthouses in the town with this, the best known one, being opened in 1852 having been designed by Stewart Gordon, the County Surveyor of the time.

With thanks to John F. Hickey

Local Directory
and Sponsors

We would like to take this opportunity to
express our thanks to the following businesses
and organisations without whose help and
support this book would not have
been possible.

Bushmills (STD code 012657)

Hotel
BEACH HOUSE HOTEL
61 BEACH ROAD, PORTBALLINTRAE   31214   31664

Insurances and Estate Agent
LINDSAY SHANKS
69 MAIN STREET   31657   32342

Self-Catering Accommodation
OLD BALLYNESS COTTAGES
36 CASTLECAT ROAD   31252

Whiskey Distiller & Bottlers
OLD BUSHMILLIS DISTILLERY CO. LTD.
BUSHMILLS   31521   31339

Portrush (STD code 01265)

CDs, Videos, Tapes, Toys, Gifts, etc .
GRAHAMS GIFT SHOP
48-50 MAIN STREET   52625   825125

Children's Indoor Adventure Playground and Restaurant
FANTASY ISLAND
2-8 KERR STREET   823595   823624

Hotel
MAGHERABUOY HOUSE HOTEL
41 MAGHERABOY ROAD   823507   824687

Specialists in Ice Cream, Coffee and Pizzas
MORELLI CAPPUCCINO'S OF PORTRUSH
7 EGLINTON STREET   824848   824761

Portstewart (STD code 01265)

Newsagent
MCINTYRE
60 THE PROMENADE   832788   834200
Also 5 High Street, Ballymoney (012656)   62168

Portstewart (STD code 01265)	Tel	Fax
Restaurant/Ice Cream Parlour		
MORELLI'S (PORTSTEWART)		
THE PROMENADE	832150	832150
Coleraine (STD code 01265)		
Accountants		
H. WILSON GORDON & CO.		
1B WATERSIDE	42164	51160
Agricultural Machinery		
GILPIN FARM MACHINERY		
234 DRUMCROONE ROAD	42900	52189
Art Gallery		
TODD GALLERY		
35 KINGSGATE STREET	53219	
Auctioneers and Property Agents		
MCAFEE PROPERTIES		
32 NEW ROW	42224	52666
Also 21 Main Street, Ballymoney (012656)	67676	67666
Bookshop		
BOOKENDS		
10 SOCIETY STREET	43300	
Charity		
THE HONOURABLE THE IRISH SOCIETY		
54 CASTLEROE ROAD	44796	56527
Fashion Retailer		
TWEEDY ACHESON		
34 THE DIAMOND	42166	58058
Footwear Retailer		
BISHOPS FOOTWEAR LIMITED		
THE DIAMOND	42465/44957	42414
Garden Centre		
COLERAINE GARDEN CENTRE		
255 DUNHILL ROAD	57972	57972

Continued over

Coleraine (STD code 01265)

	Tel	Fax

Newsagent and Bookshop
COLERAINE BOOKS AND NEWS
12 BRIDGE STREET — 44211

Scenic Videos including The Causeway Coast and Glens of Antrim
O B VIDEO PRODUCTIONS
238 ISLANDMORE CRESCENT — 823614

Solicitor
JOHN F. HICKEY
DUNMORE CHAMBERS, 2-4 DUNMORE ST. — 43244 — 320338

Travel Agent and Specialist Long-haul Travel Consultant
INSURANCE AND TRAVEL
26-28 KINGSGATE STREET — 42277 — 53421

Also 25 Church Street, Ballymoney (012656) — 62277 — 62277
and 49 The Promenade, Portstewart — 832277 — 836636

Open Diary

This section is provided to record personal
dates such as birthdays, anniversaries and
other important annual events.

January

1	*16*
2	*17*
3	*18*
4	*19*
5	*20*
6	*21*
7	*22*
8	*23*
9	*24*
10	*25*
11	*26*
12	*27*
13	*28*
14	*29*
15	*30*
	31

February

1	16
2	17
3	18
4	19
5	20
6	21
7	22
8	23
9	24
10	25
11	26
12	27
13	28
14	29
15	

March

1	16
2	17
3	18
4	19
5	20
6	21
7	22
8	23
9	24
10	25
11	26
12	27
13	28
14	29
15	30
	31

April

1	16
2	17
3	18
4	19
5	20
6	21
7	22
8	23
9	24
10	25
11	26
12	27
13	28
14	29
15	30

May

1	16
2	17
3	18
4	19
5	20
6	21
7	22
8	23
9	24
10	25
11	26
12	27
13	28
14	29
15	30
	31

June

1	16
2	17
3	18
4	19
5	20
6	21
7	22
8	23
9	24
10	25
11	26
12	27
13	28
14	29
15	30

July

1 ....

2 ....

3 ....

4 ....

5 ....

6 ....

7 ....

8 ....

9 ....

10 ....

11 ....

12 ....

13 ....

14 ....

15 ....

16 ....

17 ....

18 ....

19 ....

20 ....

21 ....

22 ....

23 ....

24 ....

25 ....

26 ....

27 ....

28 ....

29 ....

30 ....

31 ....

August

1 ....
2 ....
3 ....
4 ....
5 ....
6 ....
7 ....
8 ....
9 ....
10 ....
11 ....
12 ....
13 ....
14 ....
15 ....

16 ....
17 ....
18 ....
19 ....
20 ....
21 ....
22 ....
23 ....
24 ....
25 ....
26 ....
27 ....
28 ....
29 ....
30 ....
31 ....

September

1	16
2	17
3	18
4	19
5	20
6	21
7	22
8	23
9	24
10	25
11	26
12	27
13	28
14	29
15	30

October

1

2

3

4

5

6

7

8

9

10

11

12

13

14

15

16

17

18

19

20

21

22

23

24

25

26

27

28

29

30

31

November

1	16
2	17
3	18
4	19
5	20
6	21
7	22
8	23
9	24
10	25
11	26
12	27
13	28
14	29
15	30

December

1	16
2	17
3	18
4	19
5	20
6	21
7	22
8	23
9	24
10	25
11	26
12	27
13	28
14	29
15	30
	31

Cottage

Publications

Dear Reader

We hope you have found this book both enjoyable and useful. If you feel that it could have been improved in any way do please let us know.

This book is one of our 'Illustrated History and Companion' range. Other towns and areas currently featured in this range include:–

Ballycastle and the Heart of the Glens
Ballymena
Ballymoney
Bangor
City of Derry
Donaghadee
Hillsborough
Holywood
Larne and the Road to the Glens
Newtownards

If you require more information call us on 01247 883876 or write to:– **Cottage Publications**
15 Ballyhay Road
Donaghadee, Co. Down
N. Ireland
BT21 0NG

Timothy S Johnston